HANDY HEALTH GUIDE TO DYSLEXIA

Alvin and Virginia Silverstein
and Laura Silverstein Nunn

Enslow Publishers, Inc.
40 Industrial Road
Box 398
Berkeley Heights, NJ 07922
USA
http://www.enslow.com

Original edition published as *Dyslexia* in 2001.

Library of Congress Cataloging-in-Publication Data

Silverstein, Alvin.
Handy health guide to dyslexia / by Alvin and Virginia Silverstein and Laura Silverstein Nunn.
pages cm. — (Handy health guides)
 Summary: "Find out what dyslexia is, how it is diagnosed, and how it is treated"— Provided by publisher.
Includes bibliographical references and index.
 ISBN 978-0-7660-4276-6
 1. Dyslexia—Juvenile literature. I. Silverstein, Virginia B. II. Nunn, Laura Silverstein. III. Title.
 RC394.W6S542 2014
 616.85'53—dc23
                                      2012041453
Future editions:
Paperback ISBN: 978-1-4644-0495-5
EPUB ISBN: 978-1-4645-1256-8
Single-User PDF ISBN: 978-1-4646-1256-5
Multi-User PDF ISBN: 978-0-7660-5888-0

Printed in the United States of America

052013 Lake Book Manufacturing, Inc., Melrose Park, IL

10 9 8 7 6 5 4 3 2 1

To Our Readers: We have done our best to make sure all Internet Addresses in this book were active and appropriate when we went to press. However, the author and the publisher have no control over and assume no liability for the material available on those Internet sites or on other Web sites they may link to. Any comments or suggestions can be sent by e-mail to comments@enslow.com or to the address on the back cover.

♻ Enslow Publishers, Inc., is committed to printing our books on recycled paper. The paper in every book contains 10% to 30% post-consumer waste (PCW). The cover board on the outside of each book contains 100% PCW. Our goal is to do our part to help young people and the environment too!

Illustration Credits: Ariel Duhon/Photos.com, p. 40; © David Young-Wolff/PhotoEdit, p. 16; @ iStockphoto.com/CGinspiration, p. 24; @ iStockphoto.com/Tomacco, p. 22; Katerina Stepanova/Photos.com, p. 25; © Michael Newman/PhotoEdit, p. 14; Petro Feketa/Photos.com, p. 42; Photo Researchers, Inc., p. 30; Shutterstock.com, pp. 1, 3, 4, 7, 8, 10, 17, 21, 23, 28, 33, 34, 35, 41, 43; Simone van den Berg/Photos.com, p. 29; © Spencer Grant /PhotoEdit, pp. 13, 36, 37; Stockbyte/Photos.com, p. 6.

Cover Photo: Shutterstock.com (all images)

CONTENTS

Everyone gets distracted at times while reading. But sometimes it is a symptom of dyslexia.

1

READING PROBLEMS

Do you have trouble reading? Maybe you are easily distracted and lose your place. Or maybe you have trouble remembering what you've just read. Does your handwriting ever get so sloppy that your teacher can't make out what you wrote? Have you ever misspelled words because you were careless or because you just forgot the correct spelling?

Everybody makes mistakes like these from time to time. It's perfectly normal. Most people can usually catch their errors right away and correct them. But some people may have reading and writing problems like these all the time. It's not because they are lazy or stupid. It's because they have a learning disability called dyslexia. Dyslexia is the most common type of learning

Learning to Read

When did you learn your ABCs and 1-2-3s? Most kids learn to read by the first grade. It doesn't just happen overnight. Becoming a good reader is a process that takes time—years, even. In order to understand dyslexia, it is important to understand what steps are involved in learning how to read:

1. Learn how speech sounds make up words.
2. Pay attention to printed letters and words.
3. Connect speech sounds to letters.
4. Combine letter sounds smoothly into words.
5. Move the eyes to follow the lines of print.
6. Create mental images and ideas.
7. Compare new information with what is already known.
8. Remember what you read.

Kids with dyslexia have trouble with the first few steps. That makes it even harder to get through the rest of the steps. Not being able to connect words and letters with their sounds makes it impossible for dyslexics to understand what they are reading.

disability—a condition that makes it difficult to learn. Millions of people in the United States have learning disabilities—80 to 85 percent of them have dyslexia.

Dyslexia is not just about seeing words and letters backwards. In fact, not all people with dyslexia have a problem with reversing letters and numbers. Dyslexia affects many other areas as well. It is a condition that makes it hard for people to read, write, spell, speak, and listen. Dyslexics—people who have dyslexia—cannot figure out language the way most people do. Their brain has trouble making the connection between the way letters look on a page and the sounds of words. As a result, people with this condition may not be able to understand what words and sentences mean when they try to read.

Kids with dyslexia can have a very difficult time in school. They may think they are stupid, even though they actually may be very smart. After trying and failing many

Even if school seems difficult and frustrating sometimes, don't give up.

Individual attention can help a person who has trouble learning to read.

times, some just give up trying to learn. Some may develop behavior problems, disrupting the class and making it difficult for other kids to learn.

That's why it's so important to identify kids who are having reading or learning problems as early as possible. If you or someone you know has dyslexia, there are things that can be done to help. Experts have worked out ways to make learning easier for dyslexics. There are tricks dyslexics can use to train their brains to make sense out of the words they read.

Read on to find out more about dyslexia. You'll find out what causes dyslexia and learn how reading problems can be overcome.

2

WHO HAS DYSLEXIA?

Dyslexia affects up to 20 percent of the people living in the United States. In fact, there is probably someone in your class at school who has dyslexia. Experts say that it affects 1 out of 5 schoolchildren.

Anyone can have dyslexia. It affects people of all races and all nationalities. Dyslexia is detected more often in boys, but the condition actually affects about the same number of girls. Boys with learning problems tend to misbehave in class so they are identified by teachers more often. Girls with learning problems, on the other hand, tend to keep to themselves and do not attract attention.

Dyslexia is often inherited. People who have dyslexia are born with it. You are more likely to develop dyslexia

Can You Grow Out of It?

No. Kids who have dyslexia do not "grow out of it." The problem does not disappear when they become adults. It is a condition they will have to cope with for the rest of their lives. Adults with dyslexia often have trouble dealing with their jobs and people at work.

if one of your parents, grandparents, aunts, uncles, or some other family member has it. Scientists have found that certain genes may make some people more likely to develop the condition. Genes are very small structures that carry traits passed on from parents to children.

Dyslexics may feel stupid when they have problems learning in school, but there is actually no link between dyslexia and intelligence. Many dyslexics are very smart and creative. You might be surprised to know that people with dyslexia have become successful doctors, teachers, writers, lawyers, movie stars, and athletes.

Some of the most important and famous people in history had dyslexia. For example, the scientist Albert

Einstein, one of world's greatest geniuses, had dyslexia.
So did Thomas Edison, who invented the electric light,
and Alexander Graham Bell, the inventor of the
telephone. United States President Woodrow Wilson
had dyslexia too—and before he became president, he
was a college professor.

Handy Healthy Fact

Some Famous Dyslexics
Orlando Bloom (actor)
Anderson Cooper (journalist/television host)
Britney Spears (singer)
Bruce Jenner (Olympic gold medalist)
George Clooney (actor)
Jay Leno (late night talk-show host)
Keira Knightley (actress)
Patrick Dempsey (actor)
Robin Williams (actor/comedian)
Tom Cruise (actor)
Whoopi Goldberg (comedian, actress)

3

WHAT IS DYSLEXIA?

The word dyslexia comes from two Greek words—*dys,* meaning "difficulty," and *lex,* meaning "word." People with dyslexia have difficulty in using words or language. Basically, dyslexics have trouble making the connection between symbols—letters of the alphabet—and the sounds we make when we say them.

Think of a printed page as a message written in code. In this code, each letter stands for a sound used when people speak. Most children learn to read by cracking the "language code." They figure out what the letters will look and sound like when they are put together to create words.

The sounds we use to make words are called phonemes. The two main kinds of phonemes are vowels

A specialist works with a student using a multisensory approach to spelling words. Vowels and prefixes are on yellow tiles, consonants on blue tiles, and unusual sounds are on the red tiles.

and consonants. Vowels are sounds made with the mouth open. You use your lips, tongue, and teeth to form the sounds of consonants.

In dyslexia, certain areas of the brain have trouble figuring out this language code. For instance, a dyslexic may not recognize a short word, such as "cat." The word

A speech therapist works to improve this student's pronunciation of words.

"cat" is made up of three phonemes— "kuh," "aah," and "tuh." This seems clear to most people, but dyslexics hear "cat" as one sound. As a result, they can't use the parts of the word—the phonemes—to sound it out when they see the letters.

Also, for many dyslexics, the letters that make up a word get mixed up. For instance, the word "bat" may be confused with "tab," or the word "brain" may appear as "brian." So dyslexics often have trouble understanding what printed words mean. They may also have trouble writing. They may spell words incorrectly or may not be able to express their ideas in a way that other people can understand. Other problems may develop as well.

Dyslexics Can Read

When most people think of dyslexia, they usually think of kids who can't read. That is a very common myth. All kids with dyslexia can read, at least simple words and sentences. They don't read by sounding out words the way most people do. Instead, they use clues to figure out a story. For example, they may use pictures, the shapes of words, and guessing based on the first letter or two. But they can remember only a limited number of words. Once they reach third grade or so, dyslexics can no longer fool their teachers. No matter how hard they try, they will not be able to succeed in school—unless they get help. They need to be taught to read in a different way.

The following list includes some possible signs of dyslexia:

- Difficulty connecting letters with sounds and dividing words into syllables
- Confusion or reversal of letters and numbers, such as "sing" and "sign"; or "67" and "76"
- Confusion between letters that look similar, such as b and d
- Difficulty remembering what has been read
- Difficulty spelling
- Difficulty reading aloud
- Difficulty with handwriting
- Difficulty copying words or numbers from the chalkboard or book
- Difficulty expressing thoughts and ideas verbally or in written form
- Confusion with directions about space or time, such as right and left, months and days
- Difficulty following instructions
- Difficulty rhyming

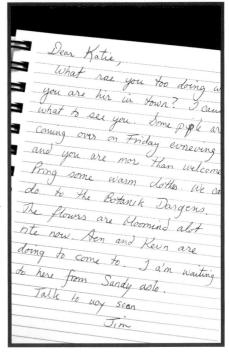

Some dyslexic students have problems with writing.

A person with dyslexia may have just a few of these problems or many of them. Every dyslexic has his or her own individual combination of difficulties. The signs or symptoms of dyslexia are mild in some people and severe in others.

Dyslexics often feel stupid because they can't read or figure things out as easily as other kids can. Their teachers may also consider these kids slow or mentally handicapped. This can greatly hurt a person's self-esteem. Dyslexics may feel that they can't handle school or the embarrassment.

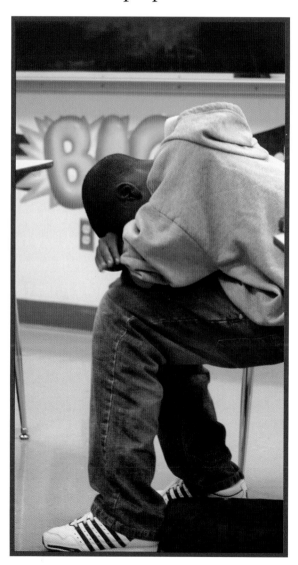

This kind of frustration can make anyone feel like giving up.

Activity 1:
What Is it Like to Have Dyslexia?

Can you imagine looking at a bunch of words on a page and not being able to make any sense out of them? You can get an idea of what a dyslexic might see by holding a book up to a mirror. You'll see that the letters are reversed. Try to read the words you see in the mirror. It's not easy. Now turn the book upside down and hold it up to the mirror. That's another way words may appear to some dyslexics. How do they look to you? Confusing? That's exactly what reading is to dyslexics—confusing.

4

IT'S ALL IN THE BRAIN

Scientists used to think that dyslexia was caused by eye problems because dyslexics mix up letters and confuse similar words. In fact, the condition used to be called "word blindness." But dyslexia has nothing to do with poor vision. A dyslexic's eyes work normally. Today, many experts believe that dyslexia develops because something in the brain isn't working in the same way as for people who read easily. The problem is that the dyslexic brain has trouble relating the images of printed letters to the sounds of spoken words.

Each part of your brain has a special job to do. The outermost layer of your brain is called the cerebral cortex. You use it to think, remember, and make decisions. You also use it to understand and form words and to control body movements. The cerebral cortex receives messages from your ears, eyes, nose, taste buds, and skin. It lets you know what is going on in the world around you.

Your brain is made up of two hemispheres, or halves—the right and the left. Each side specializes in certain activities. In general, the left hemisphere, or left brain, is the verbal half. It allows you to read and write, speak easily, and do difficult math problems. You use your right brain to read common words, do simple math problems, and understand simple verbal instructions. The right brain is also involved in artistic and creative activities. It helps you understand and appreciate shapes, texture, and color as well as musical rhythms and melodies. The two halves of the brain work together to make you a well-rounded person.

The left brain contains two important areas that help turn sounds into meaningful speech—Wernicke's area (in the back of the brain) and Broca's area (in the front part of the brain). Together, these areas help you figure out the meaning of sounds and form spoken words. Wernicke's area is involved in understanding the

cerebral cortex

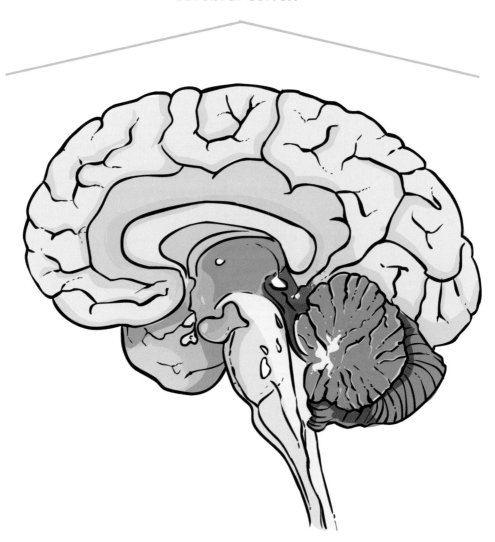

This is how your brain would look if it were sliced in half. The cerebral cortex is the largest part of the brain. It is used to think, remember, and make decisions.

Left Brain Versus Right Brain

People usually use one side of the brain more than the other. Most people are left-brain thinkers. This means they are typically better at reading, writing, and other verbal skills than at expressing themselves artistically. Many dyslexics, however, are right-brain thinkers. Although they may have trouble reading and writing, they are often very artistic and creative.

meanings of words. It also strings words together to form a sentence for speaking. Then Broca's area directs the muscle movement so that we can speak the words.

When we read a word, the vision center in the brain turns signals sent from the eyes into an image, or picture, of that word. An area in the brain just behind Wernicke's area, called the angular gyrus, turns the image of the word into sounds. Wernicke's area then figures out the meaning of the sounds. Now you can link the letters you see on a page to sounds and combine the sounds to form words.

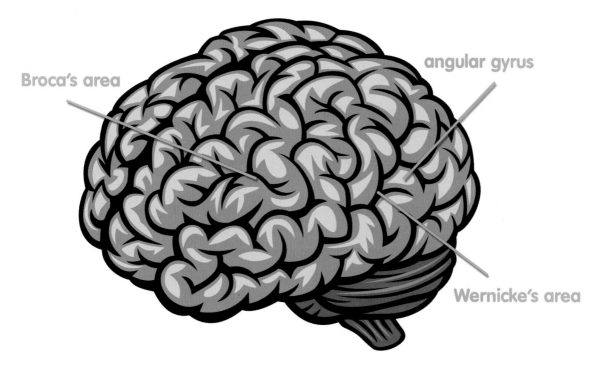

Broca's area

angular gyrus

Wernicke's area

These are the parts of the brain involved in reading and speaking words.

Researchers have learned about dyslexia by using special pictures of the brain called MRI and PET scans. These scans allow scientists to watch brain activity and find out what areas are not working properly. Scientists now know that the left hemisphere—the area devoted to reading—works differently in the brains of dyslexics.

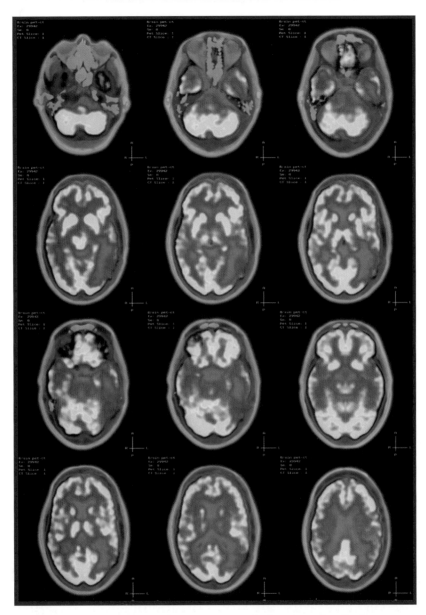

In a PET scan, active parts of the brain light up.
This scan was taken while a person listened to
sounds and tried to recognize words.

Normally, when a person reads words, there is a lot of brain activity in the language areas, including Wernicke's area, Broca's area, and the angular gyrus. However, scans of people with dyslexia show very little brain activity in Wernicke's area, the part of the brain devoted to understanding the meanings of words. The angular gyrus also has a low level of brain activity. But there is greater activity in Broca's area—the part of the brain involved in speaking words. Broca's area is trying to make up for the two language areas that are not working well.

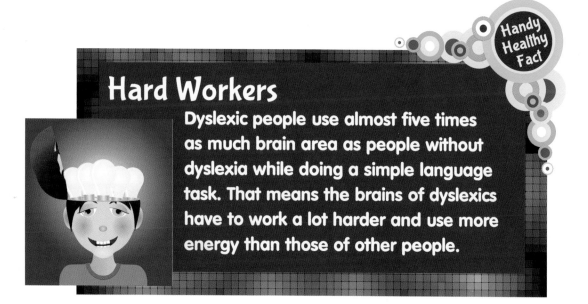

Hard Workers

Dyslexic people use almost five times as much brain area as people without dyslexia while doing a simple language task. That means the brains of dyslexics have to work a lot harder and use more energy than those of other people.

Scientists are working hard to find out more about dyslexia. They hope they can learn to identify kids who are at risk for developing reading problems. This would make it possible to catch the condition early and begin treatment before the person has to deal with any frustrations at school.

5

DIAGNOSING DYSLEXIA

It's not easy to decide whether a person has dyslexia. Dyslexia is not like a broken arm, where an X-ray can show the problem. Dyslexia is not caused by a germ that can be picked up by a blood test. That's why dyslexia is sometimes called a "hidden disability." People with this learning disorder are often told, "You're not trying hard enough." Actually, many dyslexics work harder than most people, but, for them, learning how to read is like running into a brick wall.

Many people with dyslexia learn how to hide their reading problem. Sometimes they pretend that they understand what people are saying, or they direct their energy to other activities, such as art classes or school plays. Some people may get so frustrated that they

Out of Control

Behavior problems could also be a sign of attention deficit hyperactivity disorder (ADHD). People with ADHD have difficulty concentrating, controlling their behavior, or paying attention. Some kids have both dyslexia and ADHD. These kids have a lot of trouble learning.

misbehave, which makes teachers think they have a behavior problem rather than a learning problem.

The process of diagnosing dyslexia usually starts with a physical exam. Some conditions may be confused with dyslexia. For example, hearing problems can make it seem like a person doesn't understand what people are saying. The person's eyes should be checked too. Poor vision can make reading difficult.

When health problems have been ruled out, the doctor may send the person to a psychologist or a learning specialist. The specialist will ask the patient and his or her parents questions about their family history and about the patient's behavior at home and

A person with suspected learning problems should have a complete physical, including hearing tests, to rule out any conditions that may be confused with dyslexia.

at school. The specialist may ask: "Are you upset about going to school?" "Do you have trouble with spelling or reading aloud?" "Did other family members have problems reading and spelling when they were in school?" "Do you confuse left and right?" "Do you have trouble following instructions when you're playing a game?"

After gathering information about the child, the specialist will give him or her a number of tests. These usually include an intelligence test that measures

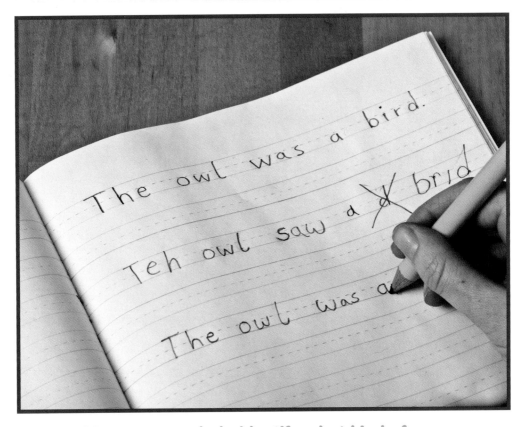

Writing tests can help identify what kind of learning problems a person has.

thinking abilities and a language test that checks the child's ability to understand spoken and written language. A reading test will help the specialist figure out the child's reading level and understanding of what he or she has read. Other useful tests may include a spelling test, a math test, a sequencing test (checking the ability to put things in the right order), and a test to understand directions, such as left and right, up and down. A self-esteem test that shows how the child feels about himself or herself may also be helpful.

The psychologist or learning specialist should also talk to the child's teacher about school performance before making a diagnosis. Getting a diagnosis of dyslexia is often a huge relief. Now the dyslexic can get help and learn how to overcome the condition.

6

GETTING HELP

There is no cure for dyslexia. But dyslexics can learn ways to improve their language skills and do better in school.

Dyslexics need to seek help from a teacher or therapist who is specially trained to teach people with learning problems. Since not all dyslexics are the same, they will do best with individual attention. They also need to be taught in a structured, well-organized environment. The more lessons they have each week, the more they will improve. With a lot of motivation and patience, dyslexics can retrain their way of thinking.

Many different kinds of programs can help people with dyslexia. Most of these programs use a method called phonics. Phonics teaches the sounds of letters

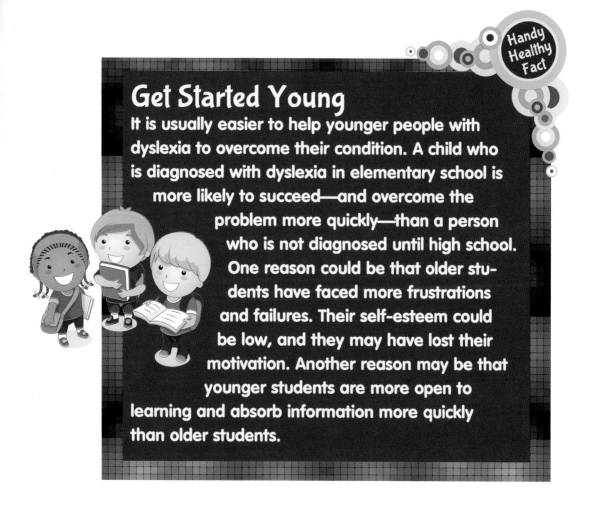

Get Started Young

It is usually easier to help younger people with dyslexia to overcome their condition. A child who is diagnosed with dyslexia in elementary school is more likely to succeed—and overcome the problem more quickly—than a person who is not diagnosed until high school. One reason could be that older students have faced more frustrations and failures. Their self-esteem could be low, and they may have lost their motivation. Another reason may be that younger students are more open to learning and absorb information more quickly than older students.

and how they will look and sound when they are put together to form words. Some schools use the whole-word method, also called the "see and say" method, instead. The whole-word method teaches students words by the whole-word sound. Some schools teach some phonics along with the whole-word method.

Experts are now starting to realize that phonics is important for all people who are learning to read, not just those with reading problems.

Dyslexics seem to learn better when they use their senses of seeing, hearing, and touching. Saying words out loud lets students hear how the words sound and feel the positions and movements of the mouth and tongue while saying them. Printing or writing words helps the students see how the letters and words look

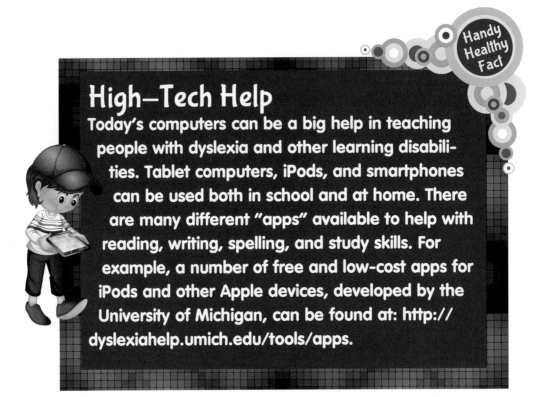

Handy Healthy Fact

High—Tech Help

Today's computers can be a big help in teaching people with dyslexia and other learning disabilities. Tablet computers, iPods, and smartphones can be used both in school and at home. There are many different "apps" available to help with reading, writing, spelling, and study skills. For example, a number of free and low-cost apps for iPods and other Apple devices, developed by the University of Michigan, can be found at: http://dyslexiahelp.umich.edu/tools/apps.

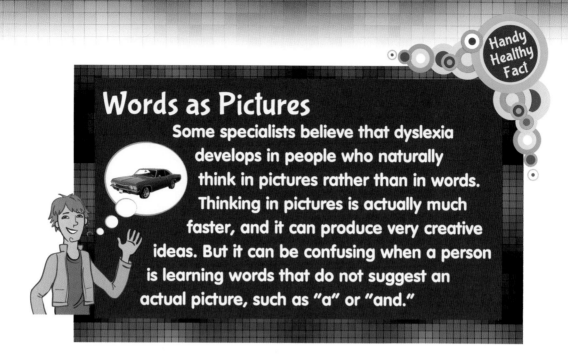

Words as Pictures

Some specialists believe that dyslexia develops in people who naturally think in pictures rather than in words. Thinking in pictures is actually much faster, and it can produce very creative ideas. But it can be confusing when a person is learning words that do not suggest an actual picture, such as "a" or "and."

and also notice how the hand and fingers feel in forming each part of the words. This kind of multisensory approach helps them to understand and remember information.

The first lesson may start with a basic understanding of the alphabet. The student looks at a picture of the letter "A," says its name aloud, and makes the sound it stands for. Then the student writes the letter in the air.

When students are learning how to form words, the teacher may use pictures of objects and plastic letters to show the relationships between sounds and letters, and how they combine to form words. For example, the

Students with dyslexia can practice spelling words that are dictated by instructors. The keyboard helps because people with dyslexia can have trouble forming letters.

teacher shows a picture of a cat. The student practices spelling the word using plastic letters, as each letter is sounded out. He or she then says the whole word aloud and writes the word "cat" on a piece of paper or on the chalkboard.

It is very important to teach dyslexics in a well-organized, step-by-step manner. They should start with

This certified teacher uses a sight word tracking sheet to help a student spell on a tablet computer. Sight words cannot be "sounded out" in the usual way because certain letters do not make a predictable sound.

Activity 2: Word Tricks

Teachers can teach young kids with dyslexia some tricks to help them remember the difference between letters that look similar, such as "p" and "b." For example, they might tell a student to think of these letters as "brother sounds" because their sounds are somewhat similar. Just as any two brothers are different, so are these letters. The letter "p" is the quiet brother, and "b" is the noisy brother. Make each sound with your mouth. Can you tell the difference? Listen to the difference between the two sounds. Feel the difference on your lips and mouth. Learning tricks like these can really help dyslexics improve their reading skills. A story about certain letters can help a dyslexic remember how to sound them out.

Can you think of some interesting "stories" that could make it easier to tell the difference between other similar letters, such as "b" and "d" or "p" and "q"?

simple ideas about language and gradually build on to more difficult information. For example, once students learn the sounds of letters, they can combine these letters and sounds to form words. They should also be able to break up words into syllables. Eventually, they will be able to put words together to make phrases and sentences.

Dyslexics can learn the same material as other students. They just need to learn it in a different way—and at their own speed. Dyslexics may have to work harder to succeed, but they can overcome their disability.

7
WHAT YOU CAN DO

If you have dyslexia, you should know by now that you are a smart person who happens to have a learning problem. That learning problem can be corrected. Hopefully, you are getting help for your condition, and you're on the road to success. Learning to read is only part of the problem, though. Many dyslexics also have trouble staying organized and remembering things. Read the suggestions listed on the following pages. They will help you listen better, remember things better, and get things done.

With the right help and lots of support, a student with dyslexia can do well in school.

- Write notes to yourself. Colored sticky notes are great because you can stick them anywhere.
- Keep a notebook with a list of homework assignments and their due dates.
- If your parents ask you to do something such as household chores, tell them to write you a note so that you won't forget.
- Use a calendar to keep track of appointments.
- Bring a voice recorder to class and record the lesson to make sure you don't miss any important information. (Check with the teacher first to make sure it's okay.)
- Try to do tasks right away. If you put them off until later, you might forget about them.
- If you have to go somewhere at a certain time, set the kitchen timer. For instance, if you have to go to practice in half an hour, set the timer for 30 minutes.
  - When you finish your homework, always put your schoolbooks in the same place. Then you won't have to hunt for them in the morning.

Get organized! Make notes on a calendar to remind yourself of important events.

- Before you go to bed, decide what clothes you will wear the next day. That way you won't have to run around in the morning.
- Develop a morning routine: go to the bathroom, take a shower, get dressed, eat breakfast, get your books, go to school.

Picking out your clothes the night before can save you time in the morning.

If you follow a routine that works for you, you may be more organized and relaxed during the day.

Some dyslexics may prefer speaking into a voice recorder to remind themselves of important dates, chores, or assignments instead of writing them down in notes. However, as students improve their language and writing skills and feel more comfortable with writing, this may change.

If people with dyslexia get the right kind of teaching and work hard, they can succeed in school. Eventually, they can feel good about themselves and all that they have accomplished.

GLOSSARY

angular gyrus—An area in the brain that turns the visual image of words into sound patterns.

attention deficit hyperactivity disorder (ADHD)—A condition characterized by an inability to concentrate, pay attention, or control actions.

Broca's area—An area in the front of the brain that directs the muscle movement so that you can speak the words once they are translated by Wernicke's area.

cerebral cortex—The outermost layer of the brain. You use it to think, remember, make decisions, form sentences, and control body movements.

dyslexia—A learning disorder that makes it difficult to read, write, spell, speak, and/or listen.

gene—A structure inside the body that passes on traits from parent to child.

inherit—To receive information passed by genes from parents to children.

learning disability—A condition that makes it difficult to learn.

MRI scan—A picture of the brain created by an imaging technique called magnetic resonance imaging. The technique makes it possible to observe brain activity.

multisensory—Using more than one sense (seeing, hearing, tasting, smelling, or touching) at the same time.

PET scan—A picture of the brain created by an imaging technique called positron emission tomography. The technique makes it possible to observe brain activity.

phoneme—A sound related to spoken language, such as a vowel or consonant.

phonics—A method that teaches the sounds of letters and how they look and sound when they are put together to form words.

self-esteem—A feeling of satisfaction or pride a person has about himself or herself.

syllable—A part of a word that contains a vowel (a, e, i, o, u, or y).

Wernicke's area—An area in the back of the brain that helps us understand the meanings of words and string words together to speak in sentences.

LEARN MORE

Books

Brunswick, Nicola. *Living with Dyslexia*. New York: Rosen Publishing Group, 2011.

Gillard, Arthur, ed. *Learning Disabilities*. Detroit, Mich.: Greenhaven Press, 2011.

Hoffelder, Ann McIntosh, and Robert L. Hoffelder. *How The Brain Grows*. New York: Chelsea House, 2006.

Landau, Elaine. *Dyslexia*. Danbury Conn.: Children's Press, 2004.

Parks, Peggy J. *Learning Disabilities*. San Diego, Calif.: ReferencePoint Press, 2010.

Web Sites

TeensHealth from Nemours: Understanding Dyslexia. <http://kidshealth.org/teen/school_jobs/school/dyslexia.html>

The Yale Center for Dyslexia & Creativity: What Is Dyslexia? <dyslexia.yale.edu/parents_whatisdyslexia.html>

INDEX

47